NEW YORK REVIEW BOOKS
POETS

DAVID PLANTE was born in 1940 and made his name as a novelist with *The Ghost of Henry James* (1970) and a dozen other novels, including the Francoeur Trilogy (1978–1982), a story of the complex relations within a family and between the family's French Canadian culture and the anglophone New England world around them. He then made his name as a memoirist with *Difficult Women* (1983; available as an NYRB Classic), about his vexed and deep friendships with Jean Rhys, Sonia Orwell, and Germaine Greer; *Becoming a Londoner* (2013); and *Worlds Apart* (2015). He has taught at the University of Tulsa; Columbia University; and the Gorky Institute of Literature in Moscow. A citizen of both the United States and the United Kingdom, he now lives in Lucca, Italy.

# David Plante

# The Death of a Greek Lover

NYRB/POETS

nyrb NEW YORK REVIEW BOOKS *New York*

THIS IS A NEW YORK REVIEW BOOK
PUBLISHED BY THE NEW YORK REVIEW OF BOOKS
207 East 32nd Street, New York, NY 10016
www.nyrb.com

*The author and the publisher wish to thank Edward Mendelson for his help in preparing this volume.*



Library of Congress Cataloging-in-Publication Data
Names: Plante, David author
Title: The death of a greek lover / by David Plante.
Description: New York: New York Review Books, 2026. | Series: New York Review poets | Identifiers: LCCN 2025038973 (print) | LCCN 2025038974 (ebook) | ISBN 9798896230243 paperback | ISBN 9798896230250 ebook
Subjects: LCGFT: Poetry
Classification: LCC PS3566.L257 D43 2026 (print) | LCC PS3566.L257 (ebook) | DDC 811/.54—dc23/eng/20250826
LC record available at https://lccn.loc.gov/2025038973
LC ebook record available at https://lccn.loc.gov/

ISBN 979-8-89623-024-3
Available as an electronic book; ISBN 979-8-89623-025-0

Cover and book design by Emily Singer

The authorized representative in the EU for product safety and compliance is eucomply OÜ, Pärnu mnt 139b-14, 11317 Tallinn, Estonia, hello@eucompliancepartner.com, +33 757690241.

Printed in the United States of America on acid-free paper.
10 9 8 7 6 5 4 3 2 1

Siede in terra...
Nascondendo la faccia
Tra le ginocchia, e piange—

—Giacomo Leopardi

This is a poem of snow falling
In a winter wood, the smell
Of resin in the gelid air,
And a deer alert and still,

The trees are crystalline,
The ice so clear the weeds show
In the current of the stream,
And no pathways or stone foundations

Left from some other time,
And no one, ever, to fell the trees,
The wind and glacial rocks forever pure
In this inviolable land, and no one there.

I held you in my arms until your body
Was cold, and I laid you on the bed
And turned to the window to watch
The night give way to day,
And I turned back to you,
Dead in the sunlit room.

My love, my love, my love.

I pressed my forehead to the wall
As your body was carried out,
And the pang came to me,
He's gone, he's dead,
The sheets disheveled,
The pillows on the floor,
And I slept where you died.

The body I held, slept with, made
Love with, that body is dead,
And death enrages me so I go out
Into the dark to find him, my lover,
And, finding him, he on his way to
I don't know where, I plead
With him to tell me he still loves me,
And he says, "No," and I reach
For his neck to throttle him
To kill him, but he won't die, he's dead,
He's dead, he's dead, my great love is dead.

Help me, Blessed Mother,
To open the door I lean against,
The door without a handle, a lock or key.

My faith in love is buried with my lover's
Filthy skeleton in a rotting suit,
And all my thoughts are base.

Help me to love still, help me
Sustain the love that was my faith
In loving him, for that faith's now gone,

And every morning I wake in the dark
That I must accept as a fact of my life,
As if I'd never believed that his love was all my life.

Open the door, Holy Mother, open up
The door, that flowers fall about me
To the floor, and I see a light from within.

The Sybil walks with me in the cemetery,
Dressed in rags, shaking her hair,
Her fists raised to the sky,
Howling, howling for me,
Lamenting my lover's death,

This my epitaphios,
Αγάπη μου, αγάπη μου,

She weeps and scores her cheeks,
And keens, kneeling at my love's tomb,
And grieves, grieves for the world dying,
Grieves for the child starving
In his mother's arms, grieves
For the ranks of men shackled
And waiting in the rain, for those
Who dig the pit and kneel around it
And are shot and fall in, grieves for
The blood of the tortured on
A school room wall, grieves for those
Machine-gunned in an empty lot,
Grieves for the hospital in flames,
For the forests on fire, the floods,
And, my love, she laments,
She laments centuries of too much grief.

A small red votive lamp in a dim church
Lights up a thin man nailed to a cross,
Illumination enough to see what men do
To make other men suffer, and for this
There can only be helpless pity,
And if there can be in pity belief
To hold us back from what we do,
The belief must rise from how far we
Rise up from where the wounded
And the dead lie in our broken fields,
And where, in cold rain, an old woman
Searches for her son, if we can rise at all.

In our bed, and half asleep, I turn
To put an arm across your waist,
Then wake up to the fact
That you're not there,
And want to drag our bed out
To where I can burn it
Among rocks at night, the flames
Casting shadows that twist and turn
To escape from me, and fly
Out high, star-wheeling as they rise.

I wake with a fine thrill when I hear
You call me from the street,
And see the bedroom door has been opened
To the landing where a light is lit,
And I rise and in a robe go out
And down the stairs to the room
Where a lamp shines on an open book
That you were reading, and no one
There, and no one in the courtyard,
Your sandals by the open door,
And no one in the silent village streets
I walk along, and I stop, stilled by
A distant cry of a baby in the cold night.

And there comes to me,
There comes over me, such longing.

He's dead, and my longing
Moves in me, moves with me about our house,
Upstairs and down, out onto our veranda,
In our courtyard, the red bougainvillea
Against a white wall, the immense longing
Forever moves in me, oh, my love,
And brings me, helpless as I am,
To the edge, where I open my arms.

Let longing be a movement in a sonata
That impels me to say, "The beauty of it
Is unbearable"—that holds me
In its thrall as that slow movement in the sonata
Played by the pianist holds back all
That is to come, note after note, each note
Straining against letting go.

I'm terrified of letting go
That will leave me with nothing to believe,
Where I will live for nothing,
And will die for nothing—

Oh, and yet, my love, oh, I live
The longing to let go.

I go on, go on, with nowhere to go,
Bereft of belief by grief that denies me
A place to go to but to kneel on the ground,
And, yes, pray for all that I do long for,
All the love I had in him, all the love I believed in.

I long for grief to mean, I long
For a poem that forgives and that redeems,
And I read back to poets who
Addressed the longings of the soul,
Poets who believed in eternity, believed in God.

I don't believe in God, but I wonder
What moves in me when Donne
Calls out to God to batter his heart?
What moves in me, moves
Without belief, and has no name,
The nameless longing for I
Don't know what, but wakes in me
The battering on my heart?

The fact is, we can't help being what we are,
Wandering in our garden in the rain
And stopping to see a rain drop on a leaf,
And in that drop the wonder of a world to live in,
All, all to belie the helpless world we live in still,
The wonder of a crystal sphere that is
Another world, a world of order and of peace,
A world of love, a world of poetry,
And, oh, the wonder, the wonder of it all.

Where we often walked together, I
Wander now, helpless in my grief,
In the grove of lemon trees,
In the shadows and the light,
And it comes to me suddenly that
The lemon grove could be poetry,
And, at a moment when grief
In its longing is to be far away
And no one there, I wonder how
Such conceits appear to us,
And I think that, yes, oh, yes, the conceit
Of the lemon grove was formed
Out in the universe, out where
The lemons are eternally bright,
There among the dark leaves,
And the lemons fallen into space.

All this I know must be, because
There is no other account of how
A poem comes to be, or what a poem is;
Or that we can conceive of
The "wonderful," the "marvelous,"
The "miraculous," and wonder
At "eternity," and wonder at "God."

Beyond belief, in the boundlessness
Of beyond belief, out there
I write my poems on "eternity," on "God,"
On "poetry," where I use such words as
"Wonderful," as "marvelous," as "miraculous,"
All, all far out there, out where I create
Unbelievable gardens, unbelievable villas,
Unbelievable towers and towns,
And, yes, oh, yes, unbelievable lovers
In their beds, and unbelievable children at play,
And an unbelievable old couple walking to their church.

Miracles occur out there, where the Gods
In their chariots rumble in a long parade,
All on their way to where the sun sets
Among bright clouds, and as they ride
The poet recalls belief in them that will survive
Their going, he standing on a mountain top
To see them as they go, to hear them sing
Their dying song, a song still heard
After they have gone, accompanied by
An Aeolian harp that harmonizes the winds,
And the poet keeps them in his prayers.

A foreigner, the poet writes in a language of a country
Where he lived for centuries with
His Greek lover, and where he writes
Without a native idiom, one that would have
Included living domestically day to day,
The table and the chairs, the bed,
The cups and plates, the pots and pans
That Saint Ignatius of Antioch dismissed
As accidents, because they had nothing to do
With the essential he was devoted to,
And so the poet believes the essential is in
A language not idiomatically his, not really,
As pure as it is archaic, addressing the Greek Gods.

The poet wants to keep his poetry
Pure of irony, as pure as prayer
To plead that the loved one will not die,
But a poem is not a prayer, and the poet
Doesn't know why he writes a poem,
And irony makes a fool of him for writing
His poems unknowingly, writing
For longing to be true, he doesn't know
To what, perhaps to what isn't possible,
Perhaps to switching on a light to see
The darkness that his lover has become.
He doesn't know what his poems mean.

The Gods have all retreated into
Poetry, where they have their own
Beliefs, and convince us that they do,
The belief that when the nymph Nestis weeps,
Her tears rise from the depths of pure
Spring water around the pupils of her eyes.

Gods perform miracles in poems, as when
In a poem Daphne, to escape Apollo,
Becomes laurel, and Apollo is amazed
To hear her singing gently through the leaves.

Orpheus rises at dawn from a bed after a night
Of making love, and dresses and leaves,
And in the market, where the sellers
Are settling up their stalls, buys
Some bread and milk, and goes home.

And another Orpheus sings again,
And loves, and weeps, and dies.

The phallic hymns, sung in procession
With flutes and tambourines, must honor
The God Dionysus, for all the nighttime
Oracular frenzy would be profane if not
To celebrate a God.

In this poem the Gods appear
In sunlight, to do what only Gods can do,
That when they depart they leave
The lawn covered with flowers,
For wherever a God once
Appeared flowers appear,
And we know that the Gods were
Where are now roses, crocus,
And violets, and iris, and lilies,
And larkspur is where, oh yes, a God once
Stood, a beautiful God among flowers.

There is so much poetry in the Gods.

Do it, believe in the Gods, that they
Calm the wild wind ravaging the fields,
That they make dark rain
Cease for sunlit ploughing
And turn the heat of summer
Into air currents that flow about the trees,
And for belief in them a beaker of water
Drawn from their river Hades
Will bring a dead man back to life.

The poet visits his friends, dear friends,
In their sacred fortress high over the city,
There where they govern with love,
And they welcome him into their court
And honoring him almost as a God
They blindfold him and crown him with flowers
And accompany him down into the city,
The city of flowers, to be greeted by all,
Men and women, where he is venerated
As a God by those who come close
For a blessing, and by those at a distance,
Diseased and in pain, calling out for a cure.

From the veranda of our Cycladic house,
On a hillside over the summer sea,
We watched the moon rise over Naxos, hot and red,
Watched the moon rise slowly in the dark
And change, for, yes, Hephaestus was at work,
Forging that immense red shield into silver
That contracted as it cooled, and, emblazoned
At the high bright center of the sky, held back
The armies of the night, or so we imagined,
As we were free to imagine whatever imagination
Allowed, and wondered: that the moon should
Be the moon, as always, and yet change.

And as for lemons and honey, those ancient
Delectables, so ancient we imagined
That "lemon" and "honey" must be eternal forms
That made this lemon a lemon,
That comb of honey honey,
As we cut large lemons on a cutting board
To make our cordial, or spooned thick honey from a jar
For our sweet, but, oh, all we ever really knew
Was this large, thick-skinned, rough, greenish lemon
With a stem and leaves on the cutting board,
And the lavender-tasting honey sold door to door
In an old jam jar by an old woman in black.

And what about our knowing each other
In our love, there, on our veranda,
The carafe of water for our ouzakia
Bright in the moonlight, the bowl of pistachios,
Our slippers loose on the marble floor,

The canvas chairs close enough that we could,
If we wanted, touch each other,
And the bats whisking overhead,
This our context and inseparable to what
We then were to each other, in that place,
At that time, you you, I I, two people in love.

What makes the changing moon the moon?
What makes this lemon lemon,
That honey honey? And what makes
Love love? Do I have to know?
Yes, I have to know, have to know what survives
Vicissitudes, what holds the whole together,
What does not die, I have to believe

That there is a moon God,
There is a God of lemon groves,
A God of beehives, a God of Love.

I want a world in my love, I want
The Greece I love to be all poetry,
So I set the poet to stand on a hill
To see triremes on the sea,
The crews singing to the rhythm of the oars
On their ways to Ionia, to Sicily, to Crete,
Where everyone speaks Greek,

And where all the world worships
Aphrodite with libations of clear honey
Poured on the ground,
And on her altar offerings
Of votive flowers, and lovers
Make love in her celestial bed,

And in my love's Greece the Gods
Look over their edge to see us
Tending our olive trees,
And milking our goats, and pruning
The vines around the stocks,
And plaiting a cage for a girl's
Pet cicada, and they hear us
Play flutes and lyres, and read our
Poems about dolphins leaping in the sea,
And the Gods like to see lovers
Lying together in the shade of trees.

If I were to have a country of my own,
That country would be discovered
In a world not yet explored,
A democracy where the governing
Would be wise, and justice and peace
Would be in the nature of mankind,
And I, hand over heart, would swear that,
As far in the future as far back to Athena
And her wise-eyed owl,
There would be liberty for all,

And I would write poetry, I would write
Of the harmony of blameless love,
Oh, wonderful the world of mortals in love,

And if in the world mortals
Turned against one another,
No justice nor peace,
And no liberty for all,
And no love,
There would be,
As Empedocles consoled,
The trees and sea and clouds,
And the fish in deep water,
And the wild animals in their lairs,
And the high-flying birds.

Poetry passes through language
After language that, each in turn,
Leaves behind its poetry, and what
Remains is the haunting language
Of the dead, from far back when
Language originated in words for water,
And stone, and air, and fire.

*Xenophanes:*

ψυχρὸν δ' ἐστὶν ὕδωρ καὶ γλυκὺ καὶ καθαρόν
cool is the water, and sweet and pure

*Francesco Petrarca:*

Chiare, fresche e dolci acque

Nothing converts from disbelief into belief
More than poetry does, offering no conviction
To prove belief, but only what hovers
After the poem is done, that sense beyond
The words that engender it, and that we read
Poetry for, so when in a poem a God says, "I love you,"
The poem convinces us that what is said is true,
And we say, "I love you," because the Gods do.

When Xenophanes wrote, καθαροῖσι λόγοις,
"Pure words," he was quoting the Gods, who are
Immortal, and so are we, who believe in them.

Restore the temple, make it grand,
Restore the gold God and the singers
And the dancers, restore all more grandly
Than before, to a world that never was
And never will be, where sunlight casts
Standing shadows of fallen columns
Across the broken floor.

For poetry, for all poetry,
Inspire me, Muse, with
Such words that inspire in me
The love of words
Far from my own language,
That another may flow
From my lips, a source
Not mine, a pure source,
Find the source in water,
In fresh, sweet, clear water,

And let our poetry be
For the Gods that they
Will come down to us
At our fountain
And listen to our poetry,
Because we know that
For poetry to be poetry
The Gods must hear.

The Sea Nymph brings wild grapes
Grown by the sea, no seeds in them
But sea foam, to share them
Among dryads and naiads.
The fawn's ears show
Above the asphodel, and the poet,
Sitting on a rock, writes a poem.

The Nymphs rise up among roses floating
On the waves, the blossoms in their tangled hair,
Their breasts bright in the foam and their arms
About one another, and, high over them, the vast sky,
Where the dawn brightens in the clouds.

The Titans wheel the sun from the sea
And all around the Nymphs splash for fun,
And later in the day Nymphs swim far away
As Titans wheel the sun back into the depths,
And boys now playing in the surf.

You try to write a poem of love,
But every poem you try to write on love
Is a trial to contrive order in the universe,
Knowing that there is chaotic disorder there,
And you put your pen down on the page
And go out into the night
To walk alone, and you look up into
The darkness where you see appear
A constellation, there, there,
High up there in spangled stars,
A maiden touches her bare breast,
And a youth throws over her a billowing cloak.

On his way home at dawn
The poet stops on the bridge
To look down on the river
In a mist, and he thinks,
Make this a poem,
Make all longing flow
In the current, and give
To the river all that is longed for
When fog raises a sense
Of somewhere else that can't be,
Because longing is a sense
That has no more than sense
For meaning, and that's all,
That's all, and the poet turns away
But turns back when he hears
Someone from the river call,
And sees in the current, flowing in
Long slow waves, long locks of hair
And a maiden rising, her hair
Dripping to her breasts, and she
Looks up to him and calls,
"Cross over, cross over."

Secondo Torquato Tasso,
Passa se vuoi vederelo,

And he crosses over on the bridge
Of gold, with high grand arches,
And on the other side he sees
The bridge fall into the river
That flows calmly on,

And he hears the songs of lovers
Hidden in the woods, and lutes, viols,
Harps, and trilling birds,
And he walks on among trees
Whose fruit, red and yellow, falls
Amid flowers to the ground.
But then he can't see, can't hear,
Now all about him dark,
And in that dark he sees a myrtle,
And in the silence he hears wind
In the myrtle's branches, and he stands
Still, as, nearby, an old oak tree
Splits open, and out dance nymphs,
And, dancing, encircle him
Singing, "Your lover waits for you,
Sick with grief, sick with love for you."
And he complains, "But my love is dead
And can't grieve, can't love,"
And they, "Look how the dark myrtle
Has become bright, look!"
And from the myrtle steps his love,
And holds him in his arms.

Traveler, rest in the shade of a pine,
And listen to the distant flute of a shepherd
In the hills, and think that, in time,
You'll walk over the hills, and not return.

Think of Iris who was light-spirited
When making love,
And dedicated to Aphrodite
A portrait of herself, a girdle
Men removed to kiss her breasts,
Her torch for dark streets,
And her magic wands.

If I came to you just to sing your beauty, Archinus,
You can blame me for impropriety, but
If I came because I had to, don't be cruel.
I was drunk with wine and love.
If this is wrong, then I've done wrong.

Andonis has a charm, a prayer
Incised on amethyst and set in gold,
Hung by a purple cord
Around his neck, and with this charm
He entices boys to leave their shuttered
Rooms the moment that he knocks.

I, Micylus of a humble nature, am buried here,
And I hope I never made anyone unhappy,
And pray the earth not lie heavily on me,
Nor the spirits keep me in the dark,
For I did my best.

He swore, Ciprio did, that he would
Only ever love her, Irini, no other woman,
But love depends upon the immortals,
Not the mortals, and Ciprio
Has fallen in love with a man,
Leaving poor Irini to cry,
As do the Megarians,
Don't count on anything.

Take my mirror, Aphrodite, take it
As an offering to you, I who mocked old age
With lovers, so many, in love with youthful me;
Take the mirror, for the reflection mocks me
For what I was, for what I am.

All things rise together, all things fall together,
As stars rise into constellations
And fall from constellations.
And what we call birth is holding on,
And what we call death is letting go.

According to Heraclitus, thought is fire,
Refined fire in the mind enlightening
Mathematics; and as thought is fire
Fire is thought, the globe of fiery upper air
Around the world enlightening the world
Of men and women harvesting olives
From old trees on rocky terraces—

Both our minds and the englobing air
Are on fire with thought,
And as fire hovers between
Water and air, potential in instability,
Unstable in potential, so the globe
And so the mind, thinking.

And as fire desires and fulfills desire
In burning, such desire and fulfillment of desire
That burns up stars in comets, that burns up
Trees, houses, temples, towns,
Desire always greater than fulfillment,
Fire's great desire to burn up everything,
So is the globe and so is the mind—

So the globe will burn up, and the mind will burn up,
And leave space, in which the final fire
Will be pure, and the mind and the universe
Will be all fire burning within fire,
For fire is eternal, fire is the soul.

You and I together,
In the mountain roads of Epirus,
Stopped at a fountain for water
From the crags spilling
Down into a marble trough,
The water fresh, and sweet, and pure,
We two young men in love,
On our way to Athens.

We were young, we were beautiful,
And we believed in the liberty
Of our love for each other, that we
Would ride on dolphins' backs
Out into the sea at sunset,
Out past the islands,
Out past the evening star, far, far out,
Never to turn back to where
We were, before we died.

We walked in the wind
Shaking the oleander bushes
On our way to the sea,
Where you undressed and dove deep
Into the waves to swim out far,
I on the rocks apprehensive
When the splashes of your strokes
Were lost among the waves,
So watched, ready to dive in, too,
And die with you, but I see you now
As I saw you rising from the sea, naked,
Beautiful, smiling at me, and then
All the dark in me opened up into
Bright light beaming around you
In your love for me, in my love for you.

I see you in your blue overcoat
In the city square, waiting for me
By the fountain overflowing
Its grand stone basin, the high jet
Blown into a mist in the winter sun.

I prepared for you a meal
You liked: first,
Cucumber with yogurt
With a little garlic and mint,
Then lamb with quince,
And, of course, a bottle of wine,
To end, a mastic pudding,
The mastic from Chios.
After, I proposed, a walk along the sea,
But if there was something else
You would have liked to do,
Such as make love, well,
We'd do that.

You showed me along the Panhellenic Way
And up through the Propylaea
And onto the Acropolis,
And, on a moonlit night, up
The steep steps of the Parthenon,
The shadows of columns cast
About us into a temple of our own,
And there you held me in your arms
And kissed me, as all your life you
Had longed to do, to make your love for me
Your history, and your love for me my poetry.

Love made our bodies more than
Naked and hairy bodies in bed,
For when blood rose in us tumescent
Our bodies became everything
That makes the body whole,
As sex must have it, must have
The body whole, must have the soul
Making love, you and I, my love, my love,
Rampant in our souls when making love.

Oh, God, that beauty should be
Ennobled in a poem, that a poem
Should be all desire fulfilled,
Fulfilled in a garden of roses,
White roses, wet with rain, hanging
Heavy on a trellis in tangled vines,

That to read a poem is to find your lover
In the garden, revived from the dead,
His rain-wet body covered with the petals
Of blown roses, is to hold him naked
In your arms, to kiss his shoulder,
To press your hand against his chest
And feel his pulsing heart,
To be roused into sex as potent

As belief in the miraculous, is to be
With him when a poem reveals to you both
A landscape lush and green that you go out to,
With springs of pure water that flow
Into pools of floating lilies, and there are
Flowering trees, and always the rising sun,
And, oh, my love, my love, the light of that sun,

The light that comes from where
Only poetry can go, and where we
Shall go, shall go and there our love
Will be eternal, with the vow
Of two lovers bound to each other
In the ceremony to celebrate their love,

Together in a pergola
With a blue mosaic dome,
Two beautiful young men in love.

When one lover dies the other dies, too,
For in their struggle for life by making love
Their love holds still for death to come
While in each other's arms.

You wrote poetry,
And when in one of
Your poems I read
το καθαρό φως
I read, "the pure light."

Love was to you philosophy,
And as there had to be an imperative
In philosophy, so must there be in love,

That the bedroom door would open
And your lover would come in,
But the door opened and no one came in,

And you asked where your calculations
Had gone wrong, so you must now go back
To philosophy, back to where love

Was the imperative that your lover
Would return to you, and you waited
For the door to open and him to come in,

Someone pure,
Someone you would hold in your arms,
Someone who loved you.

You wrote in a poem, your love was as if an idea which
you were wholly committed to, and which, if you
betrayed, would be a betrayal of everything that you
believed in.

You wrote that love was to you an inward necessity,
clear and certain of itself, and beyond
any need of proof, love most pure when you most
longed for your lover with the agonizing longing for
necessity.

You wrote in your poetry,
I pray for you in a way you never suspect except
perhaps intuitively when we sleep together. I pray
for you without knowing I pray, for when, asleep
myself, I hold you at night something like prayer
flows from me, surrounds your body in my arms.

I read your poetry, and I glory in the words
You believed in, your words, "wonderful,"
"Marvelous," "miraculous," as tortured
Political prisoners glory in the words
"Freedom," "justice," "peace,"
Words written to proclaim the wonder of words,
The wonder of your writing of the wonderful,
The marvelous, the miraculous,
The delirious light of love.

Alone and desolate, I see light shining
At the edges of the closed door,
Shining at the bottom onto the wooden floor,
And at the top onto the ceiling,
Then, slowly, slowly, I open the door,
So the beams widen slowly, slowly
Revealing the room, and I stop and hold
The door half open, the light now blazing
About the door, black against the blaze,
And I open wide the door, and in the room
An unmade bed, the sheets disheveled
And the pillows on the floor,
All beyond my own grief in the universe
Of grief, if there is universal grief
Apart from you, apart from me, in which
Universe is a universal unmade bed,
The sheets disheveled, the pillows on the floor.

I hold my head for the music
I hear, but I can't sing out
What sings within, to connect
Within without, and the unheard heard.
In pain at what I hear,
I try, I try, again, again,
To expand upon the rhythm
Of my rocking back and forth
To suddenly become music,
The music to expand more and more,
In me, in all the world,

For music unites us all in harmony with the music
Of the spheres, and no discord
In the music, which sets the seasons,
Sets the days and night, sets peace
Among countries, sets love among lovers,
And rises up high to the musings of philosophy.

Melodic modes can never be altered
Without altering the strictest Laws of State.

You and I, together, knew the secrets
Of the weather, the weather of our love,
Our sun, our sky, our clouds,
Surprising us from hour to hour,
Day to day, year to year, our inventive
Weather, inventing the summers
We spent in our old stone house,
Those summers of inventive love,
Our love all about us in a high sky
Bright over the white village
And the sea beyond, our view
Of the distant island, so close,
It seemed, we could, together, swim there,
Where we never went, but where we
Talked of going, when the weather was right.

Alone now and asleep in our summer bed,
I wake to the winnowing sea wind
Blowing chaff in waves about
The village streets, leaving the grain
On door steps and on window sills.
From so many years of barren fields,
In the drought of your death, I have
Gleaned what I could, enough
To fill the cup and in libation
Pour it into the soughing wind.

Yes, there is tenderness in grief,
In grief there is forgiveness,
And in grief there is love.
I have gathered in the grain.

Put this in: put in waking to the early morning
Chant from the church across the narrow,
Whitewashed street, and the aroma of incense.

Put in everything that made those summers
Our summers: the gathering of flowers from fields
On the first of May, and, on the summer solstice
In June, the burning of the wreaths in a fire
In the village square, and the young, and, too, the old,
Who jumped through the flames for fertility, or to dare.

Put in, put in everything, and make it all,
Oh, blessed: the fresh goat's milk
Delivered every morning, the breakfast of rusks
And butter and honey and the boiled milk
For the coffee; put in the espadrilles
On the marble floor, the tomatoes ripening
On a window sill, the red bougainvillea,
The wind in the eucalyptus trees.

Put in the doves flying out, all together,
From a large dove cot and all together
Settling into a field harvested of wheat,
Their rising all together and flying
In great swoops of flight and then
Again settling calmly into the harvested field.

Put it all in, and, oh, again and yet again,
Some blessing rises up to where

All is divined in a carafe of water
Reflecting the village and the rocky
Fields and the sea and the sunlit clouds.

From a window of our house
I saw you walk away from me,
Along a road through a field of wheat,
And I called to you to turn back,
But you went on, to where the rough road
Led up a hill, and I called, I called
To you, out there on your own.

I call out to you now, though you
Can't hear, to plead with you
To forgive me for unfaithfulness
In sex and love, forgive me
For anger, for jealousy, for lying,
And forgive me for your death,
For I never loved you enough,
And so you died.

In this poem, my prayer
To you, I plead with you
To inspire in me love,
Which only you can do,
For you are alive in me.

Love, for you, was one with belief,
And love is roused in me
That will turn day into night,
Night into day, impossible into possible
For you, for us, for everyone,
And all that I knew could never be,
Can be, and will be, and I know

That in my love for you
Is the power of belief.

Belief will shock the darkness
Of death into the light
Of life, of life and love,
And in the light you will stand
For all the world to see.

Your love was pure, and I
Long for the purity of your love,
I long for that purity.

They rise, the dead,
In the light of a summer morning,
In such light, they rise,
Led by an ethereal boy,
All stepping lightly, along
The crests of high hills.

My love, look for me waiting
For you, and, as you pass, raise
Your hand for me to come with you,
As I long to do, to go where you are going.

I've left everything to go with you,
The door wide open, and though
I don't know where you've gone to,
Leaving is a start,

And I'm on my way, oh yes,
I'm on my way, and all along
Sunshine from the rising sun
Leads to I don't yet know,
And won't until I'm there with you.

No one will believe I loved you as I did
Until I'm dead, too, because our love
Will only have its lasting meaning when
This poem is no longer mine,
Our love no longer ours, but will be
Where poetry rises up to be poetry,
And leaves us out,

Because I'm much older
Than you were when you died,
An old man now, and I am letting go,
And I, alone now, rise onto
A headland overlooking the sea,

And, there, there is everything
That was once before us, and all, all
Before me now, all there for me
To go out to, far out, into that light,
Oh, my love, oh, my love,
Out into that incredible light.

In a grassy field by an ancient road
There is a stele, and on the broken marble
The plain words carved

HE LOVED

No one knowing who you were,
Nor whom you loved.

The universe is too vast
For anything to matter,
Every murder and its bloody body
On the bed occur in the universe,
And the wonder is how

Any judgment can be made,
As when someone says, my words
Were taken out of context
For any judgment on me,
And when the poet writes a poem

Whose meaning is so immense,
There is no saying what it means,
And, too, when he climbs
A tower for the view,
Much wider than life,
Than death, than poetry,
And the universe moves in him.

I have no will, as in a sea's undertow
Pulled by the massive flow,
To where to write a poem
Is for release, to write poetry
That comes when letting go.

The poet in me cries, let go, let go,
And I let you go, my love, for you
To come back, I don't know how,
In what way, a stranger to me now,
Perhaps in poetry, but not mine,
Perhaps by a poet who sees
A gold winged eagle wheeling,
Wheeling round you, and the poet
Writes a great Greek poem
About you, you no longer my love,
But his, the poem his,
The golden winged eagle wheeling
Downwards, downwards
From a branch to the rocky shore,
And where the sea breaks on the rocks,
Lies a dying youth whom the Gods see
And raise up among the stars,
And with joy, with joy,
Naked in the strong arms of a God,
In a bolt of light he becomes a God,
Grand, grand his beauty,
The beauty of a God.

Listen, listen,

I think I hear music.

Listen

Longing is not belief, no, because
We long for what can't be, but, maybe,
Belief enough for those who long for
What can't be, and so I lean
My back against a stone wall
To look out to a field and oak trees,
And, beyond, to green hills, and then
The sky, and birds flying round
And round a stone tower where,
At sunrise, appears our Blessed Lady,
In such light that I can't bear,
So close my eyes, and say a prayer.

This poem is a walled-in garden,
And in the garden bushes of blown roses
Whose petals fall onto a rug
Spread on the lawn below, or so I write,

But the poem invents itself, and this
Has nothing to do with me,
And yet when the poem completes itself,
It seems to ring with something
Of the ring of what I think a poem
Can do,

Can make poetry of orange trees
And lemon trees, and then holly, ivy, bays, juniper,
Green all winter, and mimosa at spring,
And there are roses of all kinds
On trellises and arbors, and honeysuckle,
And in your garden you set alleys
Of mint and thyme to have the pleasure
Of their scent when you tread on them.

Help me, Holy Mother, in this.
We know there is no greater condemnation
Than we're condemned to die, but that,
Perhaps, is a simple letting go of all
That's false in our lives, when we see
You in your garden, and there teaching
Your beloved baby how to walk,
Toddling on the grass, and falling over so you
Carry him to lie beside you on the rug

Among roses, bright, bright in sunlight,
And laughter, and no dying here.

And there are trees in your garden,
Beloved Mother, for shadows and light
To wander in, and there the joy
To heare the birdes sweete harmony,
And much can they prayse the trees
So straight and high, the Pine, the Cedar
Proud and tall, The vine-prop Elme,
The Poplar, the Oake, the Laurell,
And the green turf purple all around
With vernal flowers.

Love allows me words
That when loveless are false,
And in my prayers to you, Holy Mother,
They are true, are miraculous, and cure
The suffering, and restore their faith.

Holy Virgin Mother, help me,
Revive the primrose that forsaken dies,
Give the pale jessamine color,
Make the violet glow, the musk-rose,
The cow-slips and the daffadillies
Wet with tears, and white chrysanthemum
To heap the laureate hearse where my love lies,
And look homeward, Angel,

To where we love what we don't believe in,
And in that love appears the angel,
With wide, blue wings, who rises from the patterned floor
To leave you wondering at a miracle
Conceived in you, Virgin Mother.

Oh, miraculous, all that we
Can conceive of, all that we love.

The Wild Thyme, the Honeysuckle, the White-thorn
The Pink, the Jessamine, the Wall-flower,
The Carnation, the Jonquil, the mild Lilly,
Every Tree and Flower & Herb there
Sweet & Lovely, and men there sick with Love.

Grace brings to the poem what cannot be,
Brings to the poem the Holy Virgin Mother
Nursing her son at a small breast revealed
In the folds of her bodice, and she holds
Her baby up in a beam of celestial light,
His arms open wide and laughing,
For all the world to see his mother's joy in him.

How vainly men themselves amaze
To win the palm, the oak, or bays;
While all flowers and trees do close
To weave the garlands of repose.

Your garden in winter snow, Holy Mother,
Is of white roses, and doves in bare trees,
And a light wind blows across a white landscape,
And all is white, and in the whiteness
Are no footsteps, and a silence that is kept
By white drifts against closed doors,
And you, aged and by a fire, read
This prayer to you,

Holy Mother, believe in me,
My head lowered to stone
Praying for belief—

Holy Mother, have faith in me,
In whom I have no faith.

The Gate of Heaven, the Ivory Tower,
The House of Gold, the Morning Star,
The Ark of the Covenant, the Mystic Rose.

The Gate of Heaven, the Ivory Tower,
The House of Gold, the Morning Star,
The Ark of the Covenant, the Mystic Rose.

**DANTE ALIGHIERI** The New Life
*Translated by Dante Gabriel Rossetti; Preface by Michael Palmer*

**KINGSLEY AMIS** Collected Poems: 1944–1979

**YURI ANDRUKHOVYCH** Set Change
*Translated by Ostap Kin and John Hennessy*

**ANTONELLA ANEDDA** Historiae
*Translated by Patrizio Ceccagnoli and Susan Stewart*

**GUILLAUME APOLLINAIRE** Zone: Selected Poems
*Translated by Ron Padgett*

**AUSTERITY MEASURES** The New Greek Poetry
*Edited by Karen Van Dyck*

**CHARLES BAUDELAIRE** Flowers of Evil
*Translated by George Dillon and Edna St. Vincent Millay*

**HAYIM NAHMAN BIALIK** On the Slaughter
*Translated and with an introduction by Peter Cole*

**SZILÁRD BORBÉLY** Berlin-Hamlet
*Translated by Ottilie Mulzet*

**SZILÁRD BORBÉLY** In a Bucolic Land
*Translated by Ottilie Mulzet*

**ANDRÉ BRETON AND PHILIPPE SOUPAULT**
The Magnetic Fields
*Translated by Charlotte Mandel*

**MARGARET CAVENDISH** *Edited by Michael Robbins*

**PAUL CELAN** Letters to Gisèle
*Translated by Jason Kavett*

**AMIT CHAUDHURI** Sweet Shop: New and Selected Poems, 1985–202

**NAJWAN DARWISH** Exhausted on the Cross
*Translated by Kareem James Abu-Zeid; Foreword by Raúl Zurita*

**NAJWAN DARWISH** Nothing More to Lose
*Translated by Kareem James Abu-Zeid*

**FARNOOSH FATHI** Granny Cloud

**BENJAMIN FONDANE** Cinepoems and Others
*Edited by Leonard Schwartz*

**GLORIA GERVITZ** Migrations: Poem, 1976–2020
*Translated by Mark Schafer*

**ZUZANNA GINCZANKA** Firebird
*Translated by Alissa Valles*

**PERE GIMFERRER** *Translated by Adrian Nathan West*

**W. S. GRAHAM** *Selected by Michael Hofmann*

**SAKUTARŌ HAGIWARA** Cat Town
*Translated by Hiroaki Sato*

**MICHAEL HELLER** Telescope: Selected Poems

**MIGUEL HERNÁNDEZ** *Selected and translated by Don Share*

**EMMANUEL HOCQUARD** Elegies
*Translated by Cole Swensen*

**RICHARD HOWARD** RH ♥ HJ and Other American Writers
*Introduction by Timothy Donnelly*

**RYSZARD KRYNICKI** Our Life Grows
*Translated by Alissa Valles; Introduction by Adam Michnik*

**LOUISE LABÉ** Love Sonnets and Elegies
*Translated by Richard Sieburth*

**LI SHANGYIN** *Edited and translated by Chloe Garcia Roberts*

**AT THE LOUVRE** POEMS BY 100 CONTEMPORARY WORLD POETS

**OSIP MANDELSTAM** VORONEZH NOTEBOOKS
*Translated by Andrew Davis*

**ARVIND KRISHNA MEHROTRA** *Selected by Vidyan Ravinthiran; Introduction by Amit Chaudhuri*

**HENRI MICHAUX** A CERTAIN PLUME
*Translated by Richard Sieburth; Preface by Lawrence Durrell*

**MELISSA MONROE** MEDUSA BEACH

**EUGENIO MONTALE** LATE MONTALE
*Selected and translated by George Bradley*

**CHRISTIAN MORGENSTERN** THE GALLOWS SONGS
*Translated by Max Knight; Introduction by Samuel Titan*

**JOAN MURRAY** DRAFTS, FRAGMENTS, AND POEMS: THE COMPLETE POETRY
*Edited and with an introduction by Farnoosh Fathi; Preface by John Ashbery*

**ÁLVARO MUTIS** MAQROLL'S PRAYER AND OTHER POEMS
*Translated by Chris Andrews, Edith Grossman, and Alastair Reid*

**VIVEK NARAYANAN** AFTER

**SILVINA OCAMPO** *Selected and translated by Jason Weiss*

**EUGENE OSTASHEVSKY** THE FEELING SONNETS

**EUGENE OSTASHEVSKY** THE PIRATE WHO DOES NOT KNOW THE VALUE OF PI
*Art by Eugene and Anne Timerman*

**ELISE PARTRIDGE** THE IF BORDERLANDS: COLLECTED POEMS

**CESARE PAVESE** Hard Labor
*Translated by William Arrowsmith; afterword by Ted Olson*

**DAVID PLANTE** The Death of a Greek Lover

**VASKO POPA** *Selected and translated by Charles Simic*

**J.H. PRYNNE** The White Stones
*Introduction by Peter Gizzi*

**ALICE PAALEN RAHON** Shapeshifter
*Translated and with an introduction by Mary Ann Caws*

**A.K. RAMANUJAN** The Interior Landscape: Classical Tamil Love Poems

**PIERRE REVERDY** *Edited by Mary Ann Caws*

**DENISE RILEY** Say Something Back & Time Lived, Without Its Flow

**ARTHUR RIMBAUD** The Drunken Boat: Selected Writings
*Edited by Mark Polizzotti*

**STEPHEN RODEFER** Four Lectures

**AMELIA ROSSELLI** Sleep

**JACK SPICER** After Lorca
*Preface by Peter Gizzi*

**THE TEN THOUSAND LEAVES** Poems from the Man'yōshū
*Translated by Ian Hideo Levy*

**MARINA TSVETAEVA** Three by Tsvetaeva
*Translated by Andrew Davis*

**CÉSAR VALLEJO,** Trilce
*Translated and with glosses by William Rowe and Helen Dimos*

**ALEXANDER VVEDENSKY** An Invitation for Me to Think
*Translated by Eugene Ostashevsky and Matvei Yankelevich*

**WANG YIN** A Summer Day in the Company of Ghosts
*Translated by Andrea Lingenfelter*

**WALT WHITMAN** Drum-Taps: The Complete 1865 Edition
*Edited by Lawrence Kramer*

**NACHOEM M. WIJNBERG** *Translated by David Colmer*

**LAKDHAS WIKKRAMASINHA**
*Edited by Michael Ondaatje and Aparna Halpé*

**ELIZABETH WILLIS** Alive: New and Selected Poems

**ZHENG XIAOQIONG** In the Roar of the Machine
*Translated from the Chinese by Eleanor Goodman*

**RAÚL ZURITA** Inri
*Translated by William Rowe; Preface by Norma Cole*